SPORTS GREAT BRETT FAVRE

—Sports Great Books—

BASEBALL

Sports Great Jim Abbott
0-89490-395-0/ Savage

Sports Great Barry Bonds
0-89490-595-3/ Sullivan

Sports Great Bobby Bonilla
0-89490-417-5/ Knapp

Sports Great Orel Hershiser
0-89490-389-6/ Knapp

Sports Great Bo Jackson
0-89490-281-4/ Knapp

Sports Great Greg Maddux
0-89490-873-1/ Thornley

Sports Great Kirby Puckett
0-89490-392-6/ Aaseng

Sports Great Cal Ripken, Jr.
0-89490-387-X/ Macnow

Sports Great Nolan Ryan
0-89490-394-2/ Lace

Sports Great Darryl Strawberry
0-89490-291-1/ Torres & Sullivan

BASKETBALL

Sports Great Charles Barkley (Revised)
0-7660-1004-X/ Macnow

Sports Great Larry Bird
0-89490-368-3/ Kavanagh

Sports Great Muggsy Bogues
0-89490-876-6/ Rekela

Sports Great Patrick Ewing
0-89490-369-1/ Kavanagh

Sports Great Anfernee Hardaway
0-89490-758-1/ Rekela

Sports Great Magic Johnson (Revised and Expanded)
0-89490-348-9/ Haskins

Sports Great Michael Jordan (Revised)
0-89490-978-9/ Aaseng

Sports Great Jason Kidd
0-7660-1001-5/ Torres

Sports Great Karl Malone
0-89490-599-6/ Savage

Sports Great Reggie Miller
0-89490-874-X/ Thornley

Sports Great Alonzo Mourning
0-89490-875-8/ Fortunato

Sports Great Hakeem Olajuwon
0-89490-372-1/ Knapp

Sports Great Shaquille O'Neal
0-89490-594-5/ Sullivan

Sports Great Scottie Pippen
0-89490-755-7/ Bjarkman

Sports Great David Robinson (Revised)
0-7660-1077-5/ Aaseng

Sports Great Dennis Rodman
0-89490-759-X/ Thornley

Sports Great John Stockton
0-89490-598-8/ Aaseng

Sports Great Isiah Thomas
0-89490-374-8/ Knapp

Sports Great Dominique Wilkins
0-89490-754-9/ Bjarkman

FOOTBALL

Sports Great Troy Aikman
0-89490-593-7/ Macnow

Sports Great Jerome Bettis
0-89490-872-3/Majewski

Sports Great John Elway
0-89490-282-2/ Fox

Sports Great Brett Favre
0-7660-1000-7/ Savage

Sports Great Jim Kelly
0-89490-670-4/ Harrington

Sports Great Joe Montana
0-89490-371-3/ Kavanagh

Sports Great Jerry Rice
0-89490-419-1/ Dickey

Sports Great Barry Sanders
0-89490-418-3/ Knapp

Sports Great Emmitt Smith
0-7660-1002-3/ Grabowski

Sports Great Herschel Walker
0-89490-207-5/ Benagh

HOCKEY

Sports Great Wayne Gretzky
0-89490-757-3/ Rappoport

Sports Great Mario Lemieux
0-89490-596-1/ Knapp

Sports Great Eric Lindros
0-89490-871-5/ Rappoport

TENNIS

Sports Great Steffi Graf
0-89490-597-X/ Knapp

Sports Great Pete Sampras
0-89490-756-5/ Sherrow

SPORTS GREAT BRETT FAVRE

Jeff Savage

—Sports Great Books—

Enslow Publishers, Inc.

44 Fadem Road   PO Box 38
Box 699   Aldershot
Springfield, NJ 07081   Hants GU12 6BP
USA   UK

Library of Congress Cataloging-in-Publication Data

Savage, Jeff.
    Sports great Brett Favre / Jeff Savage.
       p. cm. — (Sports great books)
    Includes index.
    Summary: Profiles the personal life and professional career of the star quarterback
for the Green Bay Packers.
    ISBN 0-7660-1000-7
       1. Favre, Brett—Juvenile literature. 2. Football players—United States—
Biography—Juvenile literature. 3. Green Bay Packers (Football Team)—Juvenile
literature. [1. Favre, Brett. 2. Football players.] I. Title. II. Series.
GV939.F29S28 1998
796.332'092—dc21
    [B]   97-22843
                                                                  CIP
                                                                  AC

Printed in the United States of America

10 9 8 7 6 5 4 3 2 1

Illustration Credits: Courtesy of the Green Bay Packers, pp. 12, 13, 17, 18, 37, 40,
42, 46, 52, 55; Courtesy of the University of Southern Mississippi, pp. 21, 26, 30,
31; Paul Spinelli/NFLP, pp. 9, 34, 50, 57.

Cover Illustration: Courtesy of the Green Bay Packers.

Contents

Chapter 1

Brett Favre leaned into the huddle and called the play. "Three-twenty-two Y stick," he told his Green Bay Packers teammates. "Three-twenty-two Y stick, on two." Favre was calling his first pass of the 1997 Super Bowl, a safe quick-out to tight end Mark Chmura, his best friend on the team.

Favre stepped behind the center and looked over the defense. He saw that the New England Patriots were crouched in man-to-man coverage. The Packers receivers to the left, Andre Rison and Antonio Freeman, were each guarded by only a cornerback. The free safety, who normally plays deep to help the cornerbacks, had inched close to the line of scrimmage, probably to blitz. As 72,300 people looked on at the Superdome in New Orleans, Louisiana, and 80 million more watched on TV, Favre was suddenly struck by a thought. Forget the safe pass, he told himself, let's go for all of it. Let's go deep.

Favre changed the play at the line. "Seventy-four Razor," he barked out, and Rison straightened slightly. "Seventy-four Razor." Rison knew the new play called for him to run a deep post pattern. Favre would try to hit him long.

Everyone knew Favre was the best football player in the world. Favre rhymes with carve, and that is what the quarterback usually did to defenses—he carved through them. He led the National Football League (NFL) in touchdown passes, and for the second straight year the league's players voted him NFL Most Valuable Player (MVP). Yet for all his greatness, Favre had one weakness. He got too hyper in big games. He tried to do too much too soon, and it usually backfired. One example was the killer play two weeks earlier in the conference title game against the Carolina Panthers. Favre tried to force the ball from his own end zone into double coverage. It was intercepted, and suddenly the Packers were behind early by a touchdown.

Once Favre settled down in big games he was fine. Although at the start, when he was a bundle of nerves and high energy, well, there's no telling what he might do. The Super Bowl, of course, is the biggest game of all. Favre was so nervous before kickoff he vomited. "Everyone says I'm nervous," he moaned on the sideline. "Heck, yes, I'm nervous. How do you not be nervous?" Then he vomited again.

There was no time to be sick now. Favre had just called an audible, and his teammates were counting on him. By trying to make a big play he was taking a dangerous chance.

At the snap of the ball, Favre dropped back to pass. Rather than run his safe quick-out pattern, Chmura stayed in to block. Meanwhile, Rison sprinted elbow-to-elbow down the field with Patriots cornerback Otis Smith. At the precise moment, Rison cut inside toward the goalpost. Favre threw the ball. It sailed high through the air, and the crowd gasped. It arced downward toward Rison, who was a step ahead of his defender now. Down it came, down, down . . . and into Rison's hands—perfect. Rison sprinted goalward with the ball, duckwalking the last few steps to the end zone. The crowd exploded.

Brett Favre looks down the field for an open receiver. Early on in Super Bowl XXXI Favre found Andre Rison for a fifty-four-yard score.

Brett Favre could hardly believe it. His first Super Bowl pass—fifty-four yards for a touchdown. You want hyper? You want high energy? Brett Favre is your man. He ran screaming like a kid to his sideline, holding his helmet high in his arm, not wanting to calm down now, and not about to. He leaped into the wild, flailing, celebrating arms of his teammates.

Favre was lucky to be playing at all. Three days earlier he had been in bed sick with the flu. He shivered under the covers with a terrible fever. "I'd waited my whole life to play in this game," he said, "and now I wasn't going to be healthy." Yet the night before the game he was so exhausted he fell asleep with the TV on and the remote control in his hand. He awoke well rested and feeling great. Highlights from past Super Bowls were on TV, and he looked up just in time to see the great Joe Montana change a play at the line and throw a touchdown pass. What a daring move, Favre thought.

At the Superdome, the players in the green and yellow uniforms were still hopping around like jumping beans on the Packers sideline when Patriots quarterback Drew Bledsoe dropped back to pass. He threw toward the Packers sideline. The pass was intercepted by cornerback Doug Evans who dived in front of receiver Terry Glenn to steal the ball. A minute later Chris Jacke kicked a 37-yard field goal to give the Packers a 10-0 lead. Barely six minutes had elapsed, and Favre's team was already ahead by two scores.

Sixty miles from the Superdome, in the tiny Gulf Coast town of Kiln, Mississippi, folks were jumping for joy. Favre had grown up in Kiln, and his parents still lived there. All week the residents celebrated. Students made cheesehead hats to wear. Town leaders planted a big "Home of Brett Favre" sign at the town line. Young children decorated trees with ribbons of green and gold. "Brett runs around here barefoot and in cutoffs," said one resident. "He's just one of the boys when he's around here." Now Favre was in the Super Bowl, and his parents and family and friends—thirty-eight people in all—were in the stands rooting for him.

Just when it seemed that the Packers would win in a blowout, however, the Patriots surged into the lead. First Bledsoe moved his team down the field with short passes to running backs Keith Byars and Curtis Martin. Then he capped the drive with a one-yard touchdown bullet to Byars. After the Packers punted, the Patriots struck again. Bledsoe threw a bomb from midfield to rookie receiver Terry Glenn at the five. On the next play Bledsoe rolled right and hit tight end Ben Coates in the end zone. Just like that, the Patriots led, 14-10. It was the highest scoring first quarter in Super Bowl history.

The Packers needed an answer. They got one from Brett Favre. One minute into the second quarter, the Packers took possession at their own 19. Favre noticed his three wide receivers were matched in single coverage. His favorite target, Antonio Freeman, was being guarded by a safety. A grin crossed Favre's face, and he audibled again, this time calling for maximum protection and Freeman to go deep. Favre dropped to pass, received excellent blocking, and let it fly. The pass hit Freeman beautifully, and he raced with it down the right sideline all the way for the score. Eighty-one yards! The longest touchdown from scrimmage in Super Bowl history! "I love the big play," Favre said. "I love to hear the roar of the crowd."

The Packers had taken the lead for good. Just for good measure, they scored twice more before the half. First Jacke kicked a field goal to make it 20-14. Then Favre marched his team downfield once more and scored a touchdown himself. From the two, he rolled to his left and looked to pass to tight end Keith Jackson. Seeing Jackson covered, Favre decided to run for it. He raced to the corner of the end zone with

In Super Bowl XXXI the momentum shifted when Antonio Freeman
hauled down an eighty-one yard pass, and the Packers regained the lead.

linebacker Todd Collins in hot pursuit. At the last instant, Favre dived to the goal line and pinned the ball inside the pylon. The referee signaled touchdown. Favre was mobbed by his teammates for his heroic play.

When the Patriots scored a touchdown late in the third quarter to pull to within 27-21, the Packers answered that too. Desmond Howard fielded the ensuing kickoff near his goal line and took it back all the way for a 99-yard touchdown. Favre threw to his pal Chmura for a two-point conversion to make the score 35-21. Green Bay's bone-strong defense stopped the Patriots the rest of the way. The Packers were Super Bowl XXXI Champions.

The first two Super Bowls ever played were won by the Packers. The team was started by a man named Curly Lambeau who worked for a meat packing company. The Packers are still owned by nearly two thousand farmers, factory workers, and business people who bought part of the team. They play their home games at Lambeau Field in the heart of America's Dairyland in Wisconsin. After the Packers

Mark Chmura is one of Brett Favre's closest friends and was a valuable member of the 1996 Packers' team.

won the first two Super Bowls, Green Bay became known as Titletown, USA. Then the Packers became losers. For nearly thirty years they never made it back to the big game. Then Brett Favre joined the team. At the young age of twenty-seven, Favre led the Packers back to the Super Bowl. After winning the game, Green Bay was being called Titletown, USA, again. "The future won't be all rosy," Favre said. "There will be other players and coaches. But I know this: We etched our place in history today."

Chapter 2

Brett Lorenzo Favre grew up in a household that was crazy about sports. He was born on October 10, 1969, in Gulfport, Mississippi, and he lived with his family in the nearby town of Kiln. His father, Irvin, was the football and baseball coach at Hancock North Central High School. His mother, Bonita, was a special education teacher there. Brett's two brothers, Scott and Jeff, played quarterback at Hancock High, as Brett did. Brett's younger sister, Brandi, was Miss Teen Mississippi.

Kiln is a tiny town a few miles from the Gulf of Mexico. The town was named for the kilns, or furnaces, used by French settlers to make charcoal. The *n* is silent and the town is known by locals as "the Kill." Brett's house is on Irvin Farve Road, a misspelled red-clay road that ends at a calm stretch of water called Rotten Bayou. The bayou was so named because trappers used to dump their carcasses in it, which caused a rotten stench. Brett's house is so close to the bayou that he could fish for bass from his porch. Alligators roam the bayou, and Brett knew to be careful. The Favre family dog had been eaten by an alligator.

Brett's grandmother, Mee-Maw, lives in a small trailer next door. Brett's aunt, Kay-Kay, lives in the house next to her. Brett's grandfather, Bennie French, once owned a bar and ran whiskey off the Gulf Coast for mob boss Al Capone. Brett's mother and father worked at the bar while young Brett would ride his big wheel around the bar stools and pool tables.

Brett was a stubborn boy. He refused to drink water from anyone else's cup or eat from anyone else's plate. He never let his brothers sleep in his bedroom and he never slept in theirs. He preferred to sleep on top of his sheets so he wouldn't have to make his bed. He was tough too. One night when he was five years old and working as a ballboy for his dad's baseball team, he accidentally walked into a player's warmup swing. "His entire forehead was one big egg," said his mother, who rushed him to the hospital emergency room. The doctor cringed when he saw Brett's injury and heard what happened.

"Must've knocked him out," the doctor said.

"Nope," Brett's mother answered.

"Well, surely it knocked him down."

"Nope."

Brett was the sideline manager for his father's football team as well. He was in charge of filling the footballs with air and providing drinking water for the players on steamy nights. By sixth grade he knew all the team's plays, including the hand signals used to relay them. "I thought the guys on the high school team were a big deal—and they were," Brett remembers. "I just wanted to stand next to the starting quarterback and have folks say, 'Look, Brett actually knows that guy.'"

Brett played quarterback for Pop Warner teams starting in fifth grade. He was serious at practice and paid close attention to his coaches. He even stayed after practice to improve his

Favre gets ready to take the snap from center Mark Winters. Even as a young boy, Favre showed the toughness it takes to be a football player.

Brett Favre grew up watching football from the sidelines. Favre's father, Irvin, was the coach at Hancock High School, and Favre would attend the team's games.

skills. He was so determined to be a football star that every night before bed he did pushups. Every day he ran the half mile from his house to the main road.

When Brett was in seventh grade, his father drove him seventy miles north up Highway 49 to Hattiesburg and the University of Southern Mississippi. Brett had watched the Southern Miss football team on TV. When he stepped inside Roberts Stadium and saw the crowd cheering the Golden Eagles he was awestruck. The game started, and Brett's eyes never left Reggie Collier, the Southern Miss quarterback. Collier led the Golden Eagles to a 36-0 rout of Southwestern Louisiana. "I saw how the crowd was going wild and I knew right then I wanted to be a part of it," Brett says. "After the game I was right in there with the rest of the kids getting autographs and sweat bands, whatever I could get my hands on."

Hancock North Central High School covers grades seven through twelve, so Brett started high school when he was eleven. He joined his father's varsity baseball team the following year and led the Hawks in hitting. In fact, he led the varsity Hawks in hitting all five years he was with the team. Brett's favorite sport was football. And like his brothers Scott and Jeff, he played quarterback for his father's team. "Of the three, Brett was the most talented," his father says. "He was rawboned, brute strength, plus he was smart. He was a natural."

Brett played wide receiver at Hancock High—for one play. "I caught a pass, fell on the football, and had the wind knocked out of me," says Brett, who lay on the field, crying, when his dad came over.

"Get up, you baby," Brett's father yelled. Brett told his dad he didn't want to play wide receiver. So Irvin Favre put his son at quarterback. That day Brett threw for two touchdowns and ran for two more. "I knew this was the position for me," Brett says. "The cheerleaders were cheering and the fans were yelling, and afterwards I felt like, 'Man, I'm really good.'"

Brett was in ninth grade when he met Deanna Tynes. "She was a real tomboy," he says, "as tough as one of the guys." Brett asked Deanna what her favorite football team was. The Dallas Cowboys, she told him. Cool, he thought, mine too. At Brett's brother Scott's birthday party, Brett gave Deanna a quick kiss on the lips and held her hands for five seconds. "God, I was sweating," he said. Deanna agreed to be Brett's girlfriend. Twelve years later they would marry.

Brett and Deanna were inseparable. They ate lunch at school together, walked home together, and played sports together. One time they were playing catch with a baseball in Brett's front yard. Brett was winding up and firing in fastballs. Deanna was squeezing the throws in her mitt and whipping them back to him. Brett's throws were getting harder and harder. Even Brett's father heard the pop of Deanna's glove from inside the house. He came outside and shouted, "Don't throw it so clang hard."

"Why?" Brett yelled back. "She's catchin' 'em."

When Brett wasn't with Deanna he was mostly thinking about football. He dreamed of playing quarterback in college, maybe at Southern Miss, and of one day making it to the NFL. He wouldn't be just another pro quarterback though. He would be the best player in the game—the MVP, the league superstar. He dreamed big, and Deanna listened. He prattled over the phone to her so long sometimes that she would fall asleep with the phone to her ear.

Brett's chances were slim, however. The Hancock High team ran the wing-T offense. It featured mostly running plays based on misdirection and trickery. Not much passing was needed. Brett sometimes only threw five passes all game.

Favre was offered a scholarship to play football at the University of
Southern Mississippi. The coaches originally thought that Favre would
make a good defensive player.

Brett did learn to be a tough player. His father taught him to run over tacklers, not around them. On defense, Brett played safety and often led the team in tackles. He was also the team's punter and place-kicker. Still, Brett's dream was to be a pro quarterback. That couldn't happen unless he first starred in college. Yet what college would be interested in him? What college knew he even existed? Three straight years he led the Hawks to league runnerup behind mighty d'Iberville High. Who noticed? Who cared? Brett was never recruited.

By the end of Brett's senior season, he knew he wouldn't be going to a major college. Scouts didn't bother to come to tiny Kiln to see him play. "Coming from down here," he said, "nobody knows who you are. No one really wanted me." Brett figured he would go to either Pearl River Junior College or Delta State. Maybe a big-time college scout would notice him there.

Three days before the college signing date, Brett got a phone call. It was Southern Mississippi. Brett's father was once a pitcher for Southern Miss, and brother Scott played quarterback there. What did the school want with Brett? Southern Miss coach Jeff Carmody explained that he had one football scholarship available. It had been returned by another player. He offered it to Brett. Before Brett could answer, coach Carmody told him there was a catch. The team already had plenty of quarterbacks. Brett would have to play defensive back. Brett did not hesitate. He said yes.

Chapter 3

For Favre, life in Hattiesburg was different. There was no Rotten Bayou to fish in. There were no big boats trolling the gulf for shrimp for him to watch. There were no Spanish moss-dangled oak trees to laze beneath.

At least there was Deanna Tynes. Favre's girlfriend went north with Favre and enrolled at Southern Mississippi with him. She wasn't going to let college separate them. And, of course, there was football. Favre attended classes and spent time studying. He even majored in special education like his mother. Yet he was in Hattiesburg mainly for football, and he knew so.

Pre-season practices began with Favre working out at defensive back. The Southern Miss coaches had seen him play in the annual Mississippi All-Star Football Game in Jackson where he played well in the secondary. They were sure his future was on defense. Favre accepted their decision. He was happy just to be on the team.

Favre still wished he could play quarterback, and after practice one day, he explained his desire to a coach. The coaching staff discussed it and declared Favre a quarterback—on the seventh string. At least Favre would get to throw a few passes each practice.

Favre made the most of his new opportunity. He threw hard and accurately. In a pre-season scrimmage against the team's No. 1 defense, he threw two touchdown passes. He threw so hard he knocked down one receiver with one of his passes. He was moved to sixth on the depth chart, and a week later, to fifth. He was making progress, but he knew he was still a long way from actually playing in a game. "I was depressed," Favre admitted. "I sat in the dorm with nothing to look forward to except practice in the morning and afternoon. I wasn't starting—wasn't even close to starting. You sit there and you think about the fact that you were a starter in high school and all of a sudden you're a nobody. It really gets you down."

As the season drew near, third-string sophomore David Forbes suffered a knee injury. Favre moved up to fourth on the depth chart. Then just days away from the season opener against Alabama, Favre moved past highly-regarded freshman Michael Jackson to third string. The coaches even put Favre on the traveling squad. He would go with the team to Tuscaloosa.

The University of Alabama has a rich football tradition. Simply standing on the sideline at Legion Field was a big deal to Favre. "I was looking in the stands and telling myself, 'Man, you're on the sideline against Alabama,'" Favre remembers. "I knew I wasn't gonna' play."

Favre almost did play. More than 75,000 red-clad fans jammed into Legion Field to watch as their beloved Alabama rolled over Southern Mississippi, 38-6. Late in the fourth quarter, the Southern Miss coaches put in many of their third-string players to give them a chance to play. Backup quarterback Simmie Carter had replaced starter Ailrick Young long before. Favre thought he might get to replace Carter, but he didn't.

Favre's chance came the following week. Young and Carter were ineffective against Tulane University, and the Golden Eagles found themselves trailing in the second half. Coach Carmody decided to gamble. He turned toward his bench and called out Favre's name. Favre would play quarterback. Fans wondered who this new player was in jersey No. 4. Favre was so nervous running onto the field he nearly vomited. Once play began he settled down. He raised his team's spirits by leading the offense on two scoring drives. Both drives ended with Favre throwing for touchdowns. When it was over, he had rallied the Golden Eagles to a come-from-behind 31-24 victory.

Favre knew all along he was a good quarterback. Now he had proved it to his coaches. Would they let him play more? Favre got his answer the day after the Tulane game.

Coach Carmody called Favre into his office. "Brett," he said, "I just want to talk to you before the media gets to you tomorrow. You're gonna' be my starting quarterback next week. I'm not gonna' draw this thing out all week, I'm gonna' go ahead and name you."

Coach Carmody was amazed at how cool Favre was. "The whole time I'm talking, he's just sitting there nodding," Carmody remembers. "He's not like most freshmen would've been, wide-eyed, saying 'Yessir, yessir, yessir. . . .' He listened and when I got through, he just stood up and said 'OK' and walked out. Darndest thing I'd ever seen. It was like he had been there before. The guy has an awful lot of maturity about him."

Just seventeen years old, Favre had become the starting quarterback for a major college program. Yet success did not come easily. On his eighteenth birthday his team met No. 1 Florida State. The fans in Tallahassee teased him by singing *Happy Birthday* as the Seminoles blasted Southern Miss, 61-10. Favre overcame that embarrassment by throwing three

When Favre was put into his first game as a member of the Golden Eagle's football team, he made the most of his opportunity. He led Southern Mississippi to a come from behind victory.

touchdown passes against East Carolina and three more against Louisville. He finished the season with a school-record 14 touchdown passes. "You wait and see," coach Carmody said after the season. "He'll be another Terry Bradshaw."

Coach Carmody was not around to see it. He was replaced before the 1988 season by new coach Curly Hallman. Favre didn't know much about coach Hallman. However, he did know what he expected of himself. As a freshman he was a "thrower." He simply dropped back to pass and zinged the ball as hard as he could, just like he used to throw a baseball to Deanna. Southern Miss receiver Alfred Williams said there were times he could actually hear Favre's passes coming his way. Favre knew he had to become a "passer." Some situations called for a bullet, but others required a soft pass. Favre had to learn to put touch on the ball.

Favre remembers the play when he knew he had become a passer. It happened against Southwestern Louisiana. Favre completed 23 of 30 passes, many of them long throws, for 298 yards and 3 touchdowns. Yet it was a short pass to Eddie Ray Jackson that was his favorite. "It was nothing out of the ordinary," Favre remembers. "Eddie Ray ran a five- to ten-yard flare to the right. There was a defender between me and Eddie Ray, and I was supposed to throw to the other side when that happened. But I just felt it. I put some arch on it, and the pass fell right in. I knew then I could do it."

Favre didn't always make a perfect throw, however. In the season's second game against powerful Florida State, Favre's first pass of the game was intercepted by superstar Deion Sanders, who high-stepped 39 yards the other way for a touchdown. Favre's team went on to lose, 49-13.

With Favre leading the way, though, the Golden Eagles lost just once more all season. Favre passed for 2,271 yards and 16 touchdowns against only five interceptions for the year, and he broke a slew of school records. Southern Miss was good enough to be invited to the Independence Bowl against the University of Texas-El Paso. Favre continued his passing assault that day by leading the Golden Eagles to a 38-18 victory.

As good a year as Favre had, he never expected what happened next. His name and picture began showing up around town. A picture appeared in the drugstore window, then a poster at the post office. More and more pictures and posters popped up. By summertime his name and likeness were plastered everywhere. Bumper stickers reading FAVRE FOR HEISMAN were on car fenders and telephone poles all over Hattiesburg.

Could Favre live up to this hype? He proved right away he could. Southern Miss traveled to the Gator Bowl in Jacksonville, Florida, for the season opener against Florida State. Favre's team usually got demolished by the Seminoles, but not this time. Favre stunned the college football world by throwing for 282 yards and two touchdowns as the Golden Eagles upset highly ranked Florida State. Favre kept it up by throwing for 303 yards against the stingy Texas A&M defense, and 300 yards against the tough Alabama defense. He was having fun shredding the college football powerhouses. "Southern Miss was a place where everyone had been rejected by the big schools for some reason," Favre remembers. "We were the Island of Misfits. We thrived on that. We'd play Alabama, Auburn, and there would be stories in the papers about how we'd been rejected by them. We'd come out and win the game, and guys would be yelling on the field, 'What's wrong with us now?' It was a great way to play."

The Southern Miss coaches were so excited for Favre's senior year that they threw away the old playbook and designed a new one for his talents. Favre was thrilled.

Everything was going his way. He and Deanna even had a new daughter. They named her Brittany Nicole. Favre and Deanna were sweethearts, but they decided they were too young to get married yet.

Then a terrible thing happened. Favre nearly died in a car wreck. It happened in Kiln about a mile from his house. Favre was driving home from a fishing trip on a warm summer evening. His brother Scott was following in another car. Favre hit some loose gravel and his car began to swerve off the road. He pulled hard on the steering wheel and his car flipped high in the air three times. It came down with a horrible crash into a pine tree. Scott smashed the car's windshield with a golf club and pulled his brother from the wreckage. Favre was rushed to the hospital, where doctors learned he had suffered a severe concussion, cuts and bruises, and a cracked vertebra. "It was like getting hit with a baseball bat," said his father. "But at least he was still in the car. Thank goodness he was wearing a seat belt."

Favre was transferred from the intensive care unit of the hospital to a private room the next day. "His liver is still bleeding and he's extremely sore," said Dr. Jare Barkley. "He needs rest. The more rest he gets, the more rapidly his body will be able to recover."

After a week at the hospital, Favre was allowed to return home for more rest. Then more trouble came. "I thought I was OK," Favre said. "I wasn't eating much, though, and when I did I was throwing up. I kept having these abdominal pains, and they started to get worse. I went back to the hospital, and they found that a lot of my intestines had died."

Favre underwent emergency surgery. Thirty inches of intestines were removed. Favre was a mess. Reporters asked Southern Miss coach Hallman if Favre would ever play football again, and the coach said, "We aren't concerned with

At the start of his senior season Favre led the Golden Eagles to a stunning upset of the Florida State Seminoles.

that right now. I told Brett to forget all that. Just work with the doctors and nurses."

Favre did work with the hospital staff as he was told. Yet he did not forget about football. "Every day," Favre said, "I tried to do a little more—whirlpool, ice, lifting weights. Gradually I fought my way back."

One month after the intestinal surgery, Favre returned to his team. He ran onto Legion Field in Birmingham, Alabama, and his teammates stared in disbelief. He was thirty-five pounds underweight. His jersey sagged. Even the 80,000 Crimson Tide fans cheered. "I had chill bumps ready to break out of my skin," Favre said. "I told the guys, 'Look, we're getting ready to whip Alabama.' They're looking at me.

Brett Favre looks to connect on another touchdown pass. When his playing days at Southern Mississippi were over, it was clear that Favre was a legitimate NFL prospect.

Stuff's falling off me. My uniform doesn't fit me. My teammates were crying. It was unbelievable."

Favre guided his team with courage to a stunning upset. Twice the Golden Eagles trailed by a touchdown in the second half, and both times Favre led a game-tying rally. With the score tied 24-24 in the last minute, Jim Taylor kicked the winning field goal. In the locker room after the game, Favre was awarded the game ball. "Not so much because he had a great game," coach Hallman explained, "but what he means to this team."

Alabama coach Gene Stallings was so impressed with Favre's courage he said, "You can call it a miracle or a legend or whatever you want to. I just know that Brett Favre was larger than life."

Favre played his entire senior season in pain, but he still led Southern Mississippi to a solid 8-4 record. When the season ended, Favre was invited to come west to California to play in the college All-Star East-West Shrine Game at Stanford Stadium. There he caught the attention of several pro scouts and coaches, including scout Ron Wolf of the New York Jets and offensive coordinator Mike Holmgren of the San Francisco 49ers. They were impressed with his strong arm and his confidence.

Favre's rating in the upcoming 1991 draft was low. Most NFL teams feared he would never fully recover from his injuries. Wolf and Holmgren, however, remembered Favre's miracle in Alabama. They knew he had the will to succeed. Yet Holmgren's 49ers did not have a draft choice high enough to draft Favre. Wolf's Jets thought they had a chance, picking thirty-fourth. Favre might still be available. Favre hoped so too. Wolf was all set to draft Favre when the Atlanta Falcons, who were one pick ahead, grabbed him with the thirty-third pick. Just like that, Favre was an Atlanta Falcon.

Chapter 4

Favre had mixed feelings about joining the Falcons. Georgia was certainly much closer to Kiln than New York, and Favre's family would not have to go far to watch him play. Yet the Falcons had long been losers. The Jets had struggled too, but they were going with a youth movement. Favre knew he had a good chance to play in New York. The Falcons already had two veteran quarterbacks, including starter Chris Miller. Favre worried that his career in Atlanta would be spent on the sideline holding a clipboard.

Favre signed a three-year contract for $1.2 million. Summer training camp began, and the Falcons welcomed their new rookie. Cornerback Deion Sanders even gave Favre a nickname. Deion's nickname is "Prime Time," and he began calling Favre "Country Time." Favre liked the nickname. He didn't like much else though. He hardly got to throw in practice. And when the season started, he was asked to hold the clipboard, just as he feared.

Favre got bored. He didn't care about practice. He didn't pay attention in meetings. When he showed up late for the

Favre was drafted by the Atlanta Falcons in the second round of the 1991 NFL Draft.

team photo, coach Jerry Glanville fined him $1,500. "I got trapped behind a car wreck," Favre claimed.

"You are a car wreck," Glanville snapped.

The Falcons lost most of their games. Favre hardly played. He threw five passes all season. He completed none of them. Two were intercepted. It was a lousy rookie year.

Then came the lucky break that would change Favre's life. It happened on February 10, 1992. Favre was sitting at his parents' kitchen table in Kiln, eating crayfish and drinking a beer, when the phone rang. It was the Falcons. They told Favre that he had just been traded to the Packers. Jets scout Ron Wolf had become general manager in Green Bay. He had hired Mike Holmgren of the 49ers to be the Packers' head coach. Together, Wolf and Holmgren wrote a list of players who could change the fortunes of the Packers. Favre's name was at the top of their list. Favre's head was reeling with the news when Wolf called. "We're excited to have you," the general manager told him. "We gave up a first-round pick for you. We feel like in a couple of years you can be our starter."

Many people thought the Packers made a bad trade. "People thought I was nuts," Wolf said. However, Green Bay starting quarterback Don Majkowski was injury-prone. Wolf and Holmgren thought Favre would be a capable backup.

Favre was excited to be in Green Bay. It was a football-crazy town. There were less than one hundred thousand residents, but sixty thousand-seat Lambeau Field was sold out every game. Tickets were nearly impossible to get. Parents brought newborns to the Packers ticket office to put their names on the thirty-five-year waiting list for tickets.

The Packers coaches wanted to bring Favre along slowly. They knew it would take some time for him to learn Holmgren's West Coast offense. Former San Francisco coach Bill Walsh had perfected the complex passing scheme ten years earlier, and Holmgren brought it with him to Green Bay. Packers tight end Keith Jackson described it as "Chinese arithmetic." Favre studied the playbook for hours each night.

The 1992 season began with Majkowski at quarterback and Favre on the sideline learning the new offense. That arrangement didn't last long, however. Green Bay lost its first two games of the season. Then in the third game, Majkowski got injured. Favre rushed into the huddle. Ready or not, he had to guide the team. The Packers trailed the Cincinnati Bengals 17-3 starting the fourth quarter. Favre rallied them back. His five-yard touchdown pass to Sterling Sharpe tied the score and the fans at Lambeau Field went wild. Then the Bengals scored late to take the lead, 23-17. Green Bay took possession at its own eight, with 1:07 left, and no timeouts. All seemed lost. Still Favre refused to lose this game.

He quickly moved his team across midfield with smart passes. Time was running out. Just thirteen seconds remained. The ball was at the Bengals 35. Favre dropped back to pass and spotted wideout Kittrick Taylor a step ahead of his man. Favre fired a strike to the end zone. Taylor caught it for a touchdown. Chris Jacke's extra point made the difference. The Packers won by a point, 24-23. It was coach Holmgren's first victory. Favre was proud to deliver it for him. In the locker room, after the celebration had subsided, Holmgren pulled Favre aside and told him he had made twenty-five mistakes in the game. One of the worst was what Favre did after throwing the last-second touchdown pass. He was so excited he ran off the field jumping and screaming. However, the score was still tied, and he was supposed to hold for the extra point. With the play clock running down and the Packers out of timeouts, Jacke chased after him and shouted "Focus! We've got to kick the extra point!"

"I've got a lot to learn," Favre said afterward. "You see all these things I've got to get straight?"

Before the start of the 1992 season Mike Holmgren was named the head coach of the Green Bay Packers. Brett Favre was one of the players he wanted on his team.

The Packers learned after the game that Majkowski had suffered ligament damage to his left ankle. He would not be able to play for a month. Favre would be the quarterback now. There was no choice. This was fine with Favre. Though he didn't fully grasp the West Coast offense yet, he felt he could wing it. The following week against the iron-tough Pittsburgh Steelers, Favre threw for the only two touchdowns of the game. In the second quarter he arched a rainbow pass to Sharpe for a 76-yard score. In the fourth quarter he lofted a perfect fade pass to wideout Robert Brooks. The Packers won, 17-3.

Green Bay managed just one win in its next five games, but Holmgren liked his young quarterback. "For a young fellow," the coach said, "he's handling the situation very well. He's really a rookie because he didn't play last year. He's got a big heart, he's strong, and he has a great arm."

By now Majkowski's injury had healed. Holmgren decided to stay with Favre anyway. It was a smart decision. Favre suddenly caught fire. He led the team to six straight wins. The streak began dramatically against the Philadelphia Eagles. In the second quarter, Eagles lineman Reggie White slammed into Favre and drove him into the turf. It was a brutal sack, separating Favre's left shoulder. The pain was fierce, but Favre insisted on playing. The trainer injected him with a painkiller at halftime. In the second half, Favre could not lift his arm above his shoulder and could not hand off to the left. With five minutes to go in the game, the Eagles led, 24-21. Favre gritted his teeth and drove the Packers 74 yards for the tying field goal. Chris Jacke kicked another field goal a minute later to pull out the victory.

The Packers beat the Chicago Bears and Tampa Bay Buccaneers, and Favre was really having fun now. Reporters asked him where he got his strong arm and he said, "I always thought it was from my father, but now I think I got it from my mother. She got mad at me last summer and threw a pastrami sandwich and hit me in the head. Hard. She really had something on that sandwich." Favre felt so comfortable with his new teammates that he often played practical jokes on them. He would sneak up behind players and dump buckets of ice water on their heads. Or he would put shaving cream on the earpiece of a phone and tell a player he has a call. "Or a bunch of us would be sitting in the Jacuzzi in the training room," said cornerback Terrell Buckley, "and he would dive in belly-flop style."

Winter came to Wisconsin, and Favre played his first football game in the snow. The air was cold, but Favre stayed hot, torching the Detroit Lions for three touchdowns in the first half as Green Bay won, 38-10. "It was fun playing in the snow for the first time, especially when you win," Favre said in the warm locker room. "But my toes are still frozen."

Six straight wins pushed the Packers to 9-6. They needed to beat the Minnesota Vikings in the season finale to make the playoffs. They lost. Yet the disappointing ending didn't tarnish Favre's great year. He completed 302 of 471 passes for 3,227 yards and 18 touchdowns. His completion percentage broke the Packers record long held by the great Bart Starr. He was even picked to play in the Pro Bowl. At twenty-three years old, he was the youngest quarterback ever selected.

Wisconsin football fans loved their new quarterback. And players around the league knew Favre could turn Green Bay into Titletown again. Reggie White knew. So White joined the Packers as a free agent. Favre remembered White's ferocious hit that separated his shoulder. "Now Reggie's with us," Favre said. "He put his arm around me. He told me not to worry, that this year we were on the same side. I liked that."

Favre and the Packers opened the 1993 season brilliantly. In the first quarter against the Los Angeles Rams, Favre

Dropping back to pass, Brett Favre looks to make another big play. Favre proved to be a valuable addition to the Packers, making the All-Pro team after his first season in Green Bay.

scrambled near midfield and heaved the ball to the end zone. Sterling Sharpe had gotten behind two Rams defenders. Both defenders, Todd Lyght and Pat Terrell, leaped and tipped the ball, and it fell in the arms of Sharpe. The 50-yard touchdown play gave the Packers the lead, and they rolled on to win, 36-6.

Favre continued to make big plays. At Tampa Bay, he threw four touchdowns to Sharpe to win it. At New Orleans, he hurried the Packers down the field on a last-minute drive to set up Chris Jacke's winning field goal with three seconds left. At Lambeau Field against the Buccaneers, he hit Sharpe with a short touchdown toss with a minute left to win by three. Along with his physical talent, Favre had developed a vital quality in a quarterback—staying cool under pressure.

Favre had become a star so fast. Yet he never got conceited. He had always dreamed of being a pro quarterback, yet now that he was, it still amazed him. "One year I'm playing against Tulane, the next I'm on Monday Night Football in front of eighty thousand in Kansas City. I'm thinking 'Holy Cow, look at this!'" he said with awe. "There are still moments in meetings when the coaches say, 'We've got to protect Brett this week.' And I think, 'I'm a starting quarterback in the NFL.' Sometimes I catch myself saying, 'Are they really talking about me?'"

Favre wasn't perfect. Too often he forced passes to receivers who weren't open. Steve Mariucci, the 49ers coach, was Favre's quarterback coach with the Packers until 1997. Mariucci said Favre got so excited he couldn't help himself. "On game day, he gets so involved that he's tackling his own teammates," said Mariucci. "Brett used to hyperventilate in games. He has a tendency to be way up or way down. We want him to be steadier."

Favre's roller coaster ways showed at the end of the season. Against the Detroit Lions in the finale, Favre threw

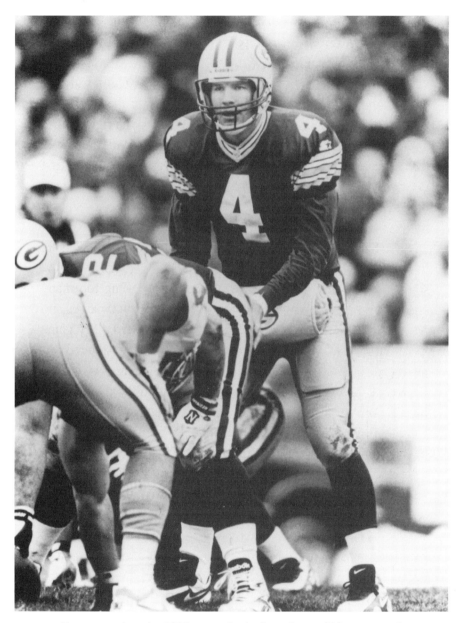

Favre came into the 1996 season in the best shape of his career and determined to win the Super Bowl.

four interceptions to lose the game and the Central Division title. Still the Packers made the playoffs as a wild card team and returned the next week to the Silverdome in Pontiac, Michigan, to play the Lions again.

This time, Favre was brilliant. With his team trailing, 24-21, and one minute left, Favre rolled left under pressure, planted himself, and heaved a bomb 60 yards to the right corner of the end zone. Sharpe had blown past his defender and was free to haul in the pass for the victory. It was Green Bay's first playoff win in eleven years, and Favre was so excited he almost passed out. "I lost my helmet, my earpads," he said. "I started hyperventilating. I was looking for someone to kiss."

The Super Bowl champion Dallas Cowboys beat the Packers the next week to eliminate them from the playoffs. With the season over, some people criticized Favre for taking too many chances that resulted in interceptions. "If I threw 540 passes and no interceptions, I'd be in the circus," he responded. "My game is to throw interceptions. And to throw 50-yard touchdown passes across my body across the field. My game is getting flipped at the line of scrimmage running the ball and getting up limping and throwing the next pass for a touchdown."

The Packers knew Favre could take the criticism. They knew he was tough. Favre's pals, tight end Mark Chmura and center Frank Winters, saw just how tough Favre was one day during the summer when they went to visit him in Kiln. The three Packers went out on Rotten Bayou in a boat. "It was a hot day, and Brett wanted to go swimming over the side of the boat," Chmura recalls. "He says we should all jump in. All of a sudden, a dead animal floats by with no head. And Frank says, 'What the heck is that?' And Brett says, 'Oh, that's a beaver—just got his head bit off by an alligator. . . . You guys ready to go swimming?'"

Favre and his pals survived the alligators, and a few weeks later they reported to training camp for the 1994 season. In mid-July, the Packers showed their faith in Favre by giving him a $19 million contract for five years. Receiver Sterling Sharpe had been clamoring all summer for a rich contract, and he grew jealous. One day at practice, Sharpe ran a deep post pattern, but let Favre's pass go over his head on purpose. Sharpe returned to the huddle and ripped into Favre. "Hey, if I'm going to run that far down the field, the least you can do is put it on me," he complained. "Somebody making nineteen million dollars ought to be able to throw a good pass."

Some players in the huddle gasped. Then Sharpe muttered under his breath, "I can't believe you're making more than me." Favre was angry and hurt. He looked directly at Sharpe and said, "They pay me to throw it. They pay you to catch it. So why don't you just shut up and do what you're told to do." Favre gained instant respect from his teammates for standing up to Sharpe.

The 1994 season was much like the season before. Favre's team won its last three games to finish 9-7 for the third straight year and make the playoffs again. The Packers beat the Lions in the first round, then lost to the Cowboys in the second round, just like the year before. Favre grew frustrated. He wondered how his team could reach the next level.

Before the 1995 season, two things happened. First, Sterling Sharpe retired. Next, Favre changed his style. He watched videotapes of Joe Montana, Steve Young, and Troy Aikman, who had won seven Super Bowls between them. He saw the three greats play it safe. If the receiver wasn't open, they threw it away. "Hey, this is no fun to watch," Favre said to himself. Then he realized they knew what they were doing. They were in control. "You've got to be boring sometimes," he decided. "Boring ain't that bad."

Chapter 5

Favre declared he was ready to take the Packers to the top. He would play under control, stay patient, and not force passes. He also promised he would not be boring.

After a season-opening loss to the St. Louis Rams, Favre led his team to victory at Soldier Field in Chicago over the Bears with three touchdown passes, including a 99-yard bomb to wideout Robert Brooks. Then he threw two touchdowns to beat the New York Giants and two more to beat the Jacksonville Jaguars. And when the Packers receivers scored, they did a strange thing. They jumped into the stands. They let the fans mob them. What kind of celebration was this?

Favre said the team was excited to be free of Sterling Sharpe. "Anybody can see the change," he said. "The team is more connected, especially on offense. No selfishness at all. Guys are excited about the other guy making a touchdown. You see the celebrations after touchdowns. With Sterling, we didn't have that. We're better on offense because we're playing as one."

Favre kept throwing pinpoint passes, and his receivers kept celebrating touchdowns. After Favre threw four touchdowns in a 38-21 drubbing of the Vikings, wideout Charles Jordan said, "He's our Terry Bradshaw. This is his team. He's the leader. He's the man."

Favre's confidence grew. On a play near the goal line at Tampa Bay, Favre's primary receiver was Mark Chmura who was open in the end zone. Instead, Favre turned the other way and fired a pass to Keith Jackson for the score. Jackson hadn't caught many passes lately and had been feeling left out. "I want to get him involved," said Favre. "We need all the weapons we can get."

In the season's last two games, Favre threw four touchdown passes at New Orleans to beat the Saints and two more at home to beat the Pittsburgh Steelers. He did not throw an interception in either game. Favre realized now the importance of turnovers. The Packers went 8-0 in the games he did not throw an interception. They went 3-5 in the games he did. Green Bay's overall record of 11-5 was enough to win

Robert Brooks looks to break the tackle of a Tampa Bay defender. Brooks and Favre share the record for the longest touchdown pass in NFL history, 99 yards.

the NFC Central division. It was Green Bay's first division title in twenty-three years.

Even Favre could hardly believe his statistics. He passed for 4,413 yards and 38 touchdowns, with just 13 interceptions. No one in the history of the NFC had thrown that many TDs in one season. For his brilliant year, Favre was an easy choice as the NFL's Most Valuable Player.

The Packers had a fun time whipping the Atlanta Falcons at home in the first round of the playoffs. Favre threw three touchdowns without an interception in the 37-20 win. Green Bay's next opponent would not be so easy. The Packers had to play the Super Bowl Champion San Francisco 49ers at Candlestick Park. Favre didn't seem to mind, however. He was so filled with confidence that he said, "In the back of his mind, I'll bet coach Seifert is a little worried." Indeed, 49ers coach George Seifert did have a reason to worry.

On San Francisco's first play from scrimmage, Steve Young threw an outlet pass to reserve Adam Walker who was playing with a cast on his left hand. Packers linebacker Wayne Simmons crashed into Walker and knocked the ball loose. Rookie cornerback Craig Newsome scooped it up and raced 31 yards for the score to give the Packers a 7-0 lead. On Green Bay's next possession, Favre took charge. He smartly moved his team down the field, frustrating the 49ers' top-ranked defense. On one play he hit Jackson for 35 yards across the middle. On the next he threw 20 yards to Brooks. He finished the drive with a three-yard touchdown to Jackson. The Packers now led 14-0. Still, Favre wasn't through yet.

On Green Bay's next possession, he carved up the defense again. He threw 20 yards to wideout Anthony Morgan, then hit Jackson for 35 yards down the middle, free and clear. When he connected with Chmura for a 13-yard touchdown and a 21-0 lead, he got 69,311 fans to open their mouths wide and yet not make a sound. By then, Favre had completed 15 of his first 16 passes. The Packers went on to win, 27-17.

"I'm not going to lie to you," he said afterward. "I'm happy with how I played today. I went up against the best, and I stood my ground."

The Packers traveled to Dallas for the NFC title game. Green Bay had not come this close to the Super Bowl since the famed Ice Bowl game at Lambeau Field against Dallas in 1967. Before the game Favre said, "Man, I think we can beat 'em, I really do." For awhile, Favre had his team believing, too. Trailing 14-3 early, Favre rallied the Packers with a pair of brilliant touchdown throws. The first was a 73-yard bomb to Brooks. The second was a 24-yarder to Jackson. Suddenly the Packers were in the lead, 17-14. Running back Emmitt Smith scored to give Dallas the halftime lead, but the Packers responded again. Late in the third quarter, Favre drove his team the length of the field and hit Brooks from a yard out. With a quarter to go, Green Bay led, 27-24. Then Smith took control for Dallas. He scored his second touchdown on a 5-yard run to give the Cowboys the lead, then darted 16 yards for another score to close out the game, 38-27.

On the flight home, Favre roamed the airplane with LeRoy Butler and Reggie White, making a pact with their teammates that if they ever got to the title game again, they'd win it.

By now Favre had gained a reputation as the toughest quarterback in football. He had started 68 straight games, the longest streak in the NFL. He had overcome many injuries to do so. He played the entire 1994 season with a hernia. He played most of 1995 with an injured ankle that later required surgery. Even when he nearly broke the ankle against the Bears he refused to come out. On one leg, he threw for five touchdowns to win, 35-28. When two Steelers smacked him and broke a blood vessel in his stomach, he staggered to the sideline and vomited blood. "Favre's bleeding," a trainer told coach Holmgren. "OK," Holmgren answered, "how much is he bleeding?" The coach knew Favre would demand to stay in the game. Backup quarterback Ty Detmer explained it when he said, "Brett's not coming out of the game unless a bone's sticking out."

Favre's body sometimes hurt so much he could barely walk. He still had back pain from his car accident six years earlier. Doctors said he had advancing arthritis in both hips. The two sections of plastic sewn into his body just below his ribs stuck out from his side like an egg and hurt terribly. "When he gets up every Monday," said his fiancée, Deanna Tynes, "he looks like such an old man."

To overcome the pain, Favre took a painkiller called Vicodin. It is administered by the team trainer and is safe in small doses. Then Favre began taking too much of it. Soon he had a real problem.

Favre's teammates did not know yet that he had become addicted. They even teased him, saying his MVP award really stood for "More Vicodin, Please." His close friends were the first to notice a problem. "You could tell something was wrong," Mark Chmura said. "He would slur a lot of his words." Chmura told Favre to ease up on the drug, but Favre couldn't.

Quarterback coach Steve Mariucci got suspicious and told doctors to monitor Favre. At home Deanna noticed signs of trouble. "I was cleaning out the closet and I found a bunch of little packs," she said. "A week later, they'd all be gone. I'd think, Jeez, that's a lot of pain pills. So I started asking him, and he got real defensive. I just kept finding stuff like that." At the ESPY Awards in New York, she noticed that he was slurring his words more as the night wore on. She asked him about it at the hotel. "Why are you acting like this? What have you been taking?" she said.

In 1995, Brett Favre led the Green Bay Packers to the NFC Championship Game where they fell to the Dallas Cowboys, 38-27. It was the first time since 1967 that they had advanced that far into the playoffs.

"I took a couple of Vicodins," he said.

"A couple?" she said angrily. "No way."

"Well, five or six," he said.

"How many? Tell me the truth."

"Thirteen."

Two weeks later, Favre got scared straight. On February 27, 1996, he checked into room 208 of Bellin Hospital in Green Bay after undergoing ankle surgery, his fifth operation in six years. Deanna and daughter Brittany were in the room with him when a nurse came in. Suddenly Favre went into convulsions. His body thrashed uncontrollably. His head banged backward into the wall. "Get his tongue," Deanna screamed to the nurse. "Don't let him swallow his tongue." As Brittany was being pulled from the room she asked, "Mom, is he going to die?"

Twenty minutes later doctors managed to bring Favre back to normal. "You've just suffered a seizure, Brett," physician John Gray told him. "People can die from those." Favre's addiction to Vicodin had nearly killed him.

Favre now knew that he needed help. On May 14 at a press conference, with coach Holmgren sitting on one side of him and Deanna on the other, he told the public his problem. "It's kind of a difficult time," he said. "Because throughout the years I've played with pain and injuries and, uh, suffered numerous surgeries, and possibly became dependent on medication. Voluntarily, I'm going to get into a treatment facility for however long it takes to get better. My objective is to get better so I can continue to play at the level that I have and to get to the Super Bowl."

At 5 o'clock the next morning, Favre was whisked by jet to the Menninger Clinic in Topeka, Kansas. It is a treatment facility for addicts. There Favre checked himself in. "One thing you have to respect about Brett," said teammate Reggie

Brett Favre has sustained many injuries during his football career. In 1996, Favre announced that he would undergo treatment to end his addiction to the painkiller Vicodin.

White, "he came out and said, 'I have a problem.' That is the first step toward getting rid of the problem. He has my full support."

Before Favre entered the clinic, he spoke to reporters. "People look at me and say, 'I'd love to be that guy,'" Favre said. "But if they knew what it took to be that guy, they wouldn't love to be him, I can guarantee you that. I'm entering a treatment center. Would they love that?"

Chapter 6

Favre emerged from the rehabilitation clinic rested and with a new realization. "When I was growing up," he said, "I thought an alcoholic was just a bum on the street. I thought someone who was addicted to drugs was just some bum who was a loser. It's totally the opposite."

Favre had overcome his addiction to painkillers. He was ready to start fresh. "I can't believe it," said Deanna, wiping her eyes. "The old Brett's back." Sixteen days after leaving the clinic, Favre married Deanna. They moved with Brittany into a large house near Green Bay. Then Favre joined his teammates for training camp.

When Favre's teammates caught sight of him, they hardly believed their eyes. Favre was in the best shape of his life. He had run and lifted weights every day in Topeka. A year earlier he weighed 230 pounds with 18 percent body fat. Now he weighed 218 with 8 percent.

Then the magical 1996 season began. In the season opener at Tampa Bay, Favre threw three first-half touchdowns to Keith Jackson as the Packers rolled over the Buccaneers,

34-3. In the second game, played at Lambeau Field under the bright lights of *Monday Night Football*, Favre threw three more TDs in a 39-13 clobbering of the Philadelphia Eagles. In the third game he threw for three more scores to bury the San Diego Chargers, 42-10. "We know we'll win a Super Bowl, we really do," Favre said. "I think it's going to be this year."

The Packers were determined to finish with the best record in their conference and gain homefield advantage through the playoffs. Even a season-ending injury to star wideout Robert Brooks in an overtime win against the San Francisco 49ers couldn't stop them. Green Bay won its last four games to finish 13-3 and clinch homefield advantage. Favre shattered several passing records in the process, including his own NFC mark for touchdown passes. He was honored as the league's MVP for the second straight year, joining legendary Joe Montana as the only two players in history to win the award twice in a row.

In the playoffs, no team proved a match for the Packers. The 49ers were the first to lose in the cold slop of Lambeau. On a day a polar bear would love, Desmond Howard returned one punt for a touchdown and another to the 7-yard line to take the Packers to a quick 14-0 lead. While the 49ers slipped and slided and committed five turnovers, Favre protected the ball well, throwing just four incompletions and no interceptions. The Packers rolled to a surprisingly easy 35-14 victory.

In the NFC Championship game a week later, the Packers played for the right to go to the Super Bowl. In conditions better suited for pigs than players, Green Bay dominated the upstart Carolina Panthers. Favre started the game with a mistake, forcing a slant pass to Don Beebe into tight coverage. Linebacker Sam Mills intercepted and was tackled

Desmond Howard was the most dangerous kick returner in professional football during the 1996 season. Because of his outstanding play, he was named the Most Valuable Player of Super Bowl XXXI.

at the Packer 2-yard line, leading to the game's first score. Linebacker Lamar Lathon got in Favre's face and said, "This is going to be a long day." Favre just shrugged his shoulders and said, "We'll see." Lathon proved right. It was a long day—for the Panthers.

Favre tied the game on the first play of the second quarter with a 29-yard perfect rainbow toss to Dorsey Levens. Then he put the Pack ahead for good a minute before the half with a 6-yard TD to Antonio Freeman. Green Bay cruised to a 30-13 victory. As the last seconds ticked off the clock, Favre threw a bearhug around Reggie White and whispered, "Congratulations, you deserve this." White could have said the same thing to Favre.

At the 1997 Super Bowl in New Orleans, Louisiana, Favre put on an aerial show. Against the New England Patriots, his first pass went for 54 yards and a touchdown. Another of his passes—an 81-yard bomb—set the Super Bowl record for the longest touchdown pass in history. Favre's Packers won the game, 35-21, to become world champions. "It's the greatest feeling in the world," Favre said afterward. "But now I'm greedy. Now I want to win more."

Favre returned home to Green Bay to prepare for a run at the 1998 Super Bowl. He maintained his strenuous workout routine of lifting weights, running sprints on the treadmill, and doing pushups with daughter Brittany on his back. In the summer he returned with Deanna and Brittany to Kiln where his parents keep his bedroom the same. The posters of Charles Barkley and Joe Montana are still on the wall, and the waterbed stays filled. Brett spent another summer in his boat on Rotten Bayou, fishing and dodging alligators. "Where else could I have so much fun," he says, laughing. "That's what this is all about. Having fun."

Favre plays football that way. He's wild and he has fun.

Brett Favre attributes his success to his desire and love for the game. Green Bay fans would love for Favre to remain the Packers' quarterback for years to come.

He goes back to pass, trips, gets up, and fires a touchdown pass. The Packers' fans love to watch his fearless style of play. "There are quarterbacks who can outrun me, probably outthrow me, ones who are more accurate," he says. "What separates me from [them]? It's the fire inside. I love to play the game."

Career Statistics

YEAR	TEAM	PASS ATT.	PASS COMP.	PASS YARDS	PCT.	TD	INT.
1987	So. Miss.	194	79	1,264	40.7	14	13
1988	So. Miss.	319	178	2,271	55.8	16	5
1989	So. Miss.	381	206	2,588	54.1	14	10
1990	So. Miss.	275	150	1,572	54.5	7	6
College Totals		1,169	613	7,695	52.4	51	34

YEAR	TEAM	PASS ATT.	PASS COMP.	PASS YARDS	PCT.	TD	INT.
1991	Atlanta	5	0	0	0	0	2
1992	Green Bay	471	302	3,227	64.1	18	13
1993	Green Bay	522	318	3,303	60.9	19	24
1994	Green Bay	582	363	3,882	62.4	33	14
1995	Green Bay	570	359	4,413	63.0	38	13
1996	Green Bay	543	325	3,899	59.9	39	13
NFL Totals		2,693	1,667	18,724	61.9	147	79

Where to Write Brett Favre:

Mr. Brett Favre
c/o Green Bay Packers
1265 Lombardi Ave.
Green Bay, WI 54307

Index